Akashic Records

"One True Love"

A PRACTICAL GUIDE TO
ACCESS YOUR OWN AKASHIC RECORDS

Akashic Records

"One True Love"

A PRACTICAL GUIDE TO
ACCESS YOUR OWN AKASHIC RECORDS

GABRIELLE ORR

To my Parents Josef and Mathilde.
Thank You for Having Allowed
My Soul
To Join this Realm Once Again.

To Those Who Know!

*There are those who don't know, and they
don't know that they don't know.
They are innocent as children, and it is for us to
nurture them, to encourage them!*

*Then there are those who don't know and who
know that they don't know.
They are willing; teach them!*

*Then there are those who don't know and
think that they know.
They are dangerous; avoid them!*

*Then there are those who know but don't
know that they know.
They are asleep; awake them!*

*Then there are those who know and who know
that they know.
Do not follow them because if they know that
they know, they would not have you follow
them. But listen very carefully to what they
have to tell you because they might say
something that reminds you of what you
already know!*

— Unknown

Contents

Part I

    Meditation
    Exercise

    What Is the Meaning of Akasha?
    What Does that Mean for Us?
    You Are Going to Learn to Speak a New Language
    What Does this Mean for You Taking this Class?

Part II

Part III

Part IV

Part V

Preface

*Your vision will become clear only when you can
look into your own heart.
Who looks outside, dreams;
who looks inside awakes.*
-CARL JUNG

Learning how to access my Akashic Records has
changed my life on the deepest level. It has opened up
my heart and allowed me to realize that I am already
"at home" and that I don't have to worry about my
path anymore because I am at my destination at this
moment. Now.

Before I knew how to connect to this source of unconditional love, most of the time I was in an internal
state of panic, fear, and survival. I constantly felt as
if I had to battle against what life presented to me. Of
course I meditated, and I studied numerous healing
practices. I connected with incredible healers from all

over the world and experienced healing rituals and techniques in several different Eastern, Western, and indigenous cultures. Not one of these ever touched my heart or opened the core of my being like the Akashic Records do.

Out of my deepest respect and gratitude toward this source of knowledge and unconditional love, I feel called to share this incredible gift with you. It is my heartfelt wish for you to feel the same love and caring that I feel when I am in my Akashic Records. I want you to receive the answers you are looking for, the healing you are longing for, and the uplifting joy and everlasting love that will propel you out of survival mode and into a state of thriving and co-creating. You are here on purpose, and you are never alone. Accessing the Akashic Records will help you discover this purpose and remind you of your connection with the divine.

In other words, how could you ever be separate from your source if the essence of this source is who you truly are?

Gabrielle Orr
Miami Beach, Florida, April 2013

Introduction

It is thought and feeling
which guides the universe,
not deeds.
-EDGAR CAYCE

This book's intention is to ignite and maintain the love within you.

It is my wish that you will find your true self in the process of working with the divine energy of the Akashic Records.

Developing a connection to the Akashic Records requires both heart and spirit. I am going to use a common medium—language—to explain the process and the guidelines of connecting to this source.

This is a workbook—a manual that will teach you everything you need to know in order to successfully access your Akashic Records.

Please follow the guidelines and instructions carefully and in the given sequence so that you will receive the most benefit from this class.

Your Intention Matters

For he that expects nothing shall not be disappointed,
but he that expects much
- if he lives and uses that in hand day by day –
shall be full to running over.
-EDGAR CAYCE

I learned how to access the Akashic Records at the perfect time in my life. I had been incessantly searching for relief and healing, and I had taken on the spiritual path without knowing the person I truly was. I was looking for something on the outside that would fill me with peace and harmony on the inside. Eventually I found it in the care and guidance I received from my Masters and Teachers in the Akashic Records. I found something in the "material realm" that enabled me to make a connection to my internal being so I could live the peaceful life I was so desperately longing for. The foundation of this discovery was the intention to thrive.

Please ask yourself what your true intention was when you picked up this book and why you want to access your own Akashic Records.

What is the vibrational calling that stands behind your physical action?

There is no right or wrong answer. I just want you to be engaged in this learning process, and the biggest and most important part is you and your willingness to thrive and live a conscious, purposeful life.

About You
and this Book

Be realistic.
Plan for a miracle.
-Bhagwan Shree Rajineesh

The pages of this book are not filled with a lot of information about me, my journey, the meaning of religion, or lots of other information that doesn't really contribute to the true matter on how to access your own Akashic Records. In that sense it's exactly like I am, straight forward and to the point.

I am strictly following the demands and guidance of my Akashic Records to get the information "out there" and to teach others how to make a connection with the realm of unconditional love. I have done this for the last seventeen years, both in person, using a group class setting, and via the Internet. Now it is time to put the knowledge into writing and pass it on to you.

It is your birthright to access this source. Everybody is able to make this connection. The quality of your connection depends on you—your intentions and the effort you are willing to put into it. Just as it would take every amateur serious dedication to become a professional golfer, you will only become a true champion at accessing your Akashic Records if you are willing to focus on your game, are committed to your practice, and are clear in your intentions of why you are pursuing this endeavor.

The information provided in this book will lead you to your own Akashic Records. You will receive everything you need to know to make the connection and to navigate through the realm of the Akashic Records with your questions. Even though I am teaching you how to access your Akashic Records by using language, you will also receive this teaching in a very high vibrational form from the Akashic Records. It is this vibrational energy that will allow you to make the connection. It will elevate your energy to the appropriate level so you can feel the love coming from them and flowing into you. This will make you aware of the whole and magnificent soul-being in human form that you are.

In other words, these pages are infused with love, and I want you—need you—to feel this love.

How to Use this Book

Everything should be made as simple as possible, but not simpler.
-ALBERT EINSTEIN

As you read this book, you will notice that your participation is needed. So please keep a pen and paper handy.

If you are the kind of person who thinks that you can usually just manage the material by reading the book, you will be disappointed. It is important for you to participate in this process fully because this is all—and foremost only—about you and your connection with your Akashic Records.

I encourage you to write down your answers to the questions because you will not be able to remember in full what you receive from your Masters and Teachers. I also want you to see that the answers you are receiving are really coming from your Akashic Records.

Rule number one: answer all exercises in writing.

Rule number two: don't jump ahead in the book. Follow the process page by page and trust that it has been designed with divine intentions. So no short cuts, please. Trust the process. You deserve to really receive this gift, and I am dedicated in presenting it to you.

Rule number three: enjoy the journey, and, to most of you, lighten up a little. Life is good, and it's about to get a whole lot better.

Disclaimer

*The wise are wise only because
they love. The fools are fools only
because they think they can
understand love.*
-PAULO COELHO

The Masters and Teachers of the Akashic Records are here to help you to work through patterns and blockages that hold you back from experiencing your full potential for growth, joy, harmony and direction.

The divine vibration received during this guidance will allow you to make adjustments in your free will for healing, change and choice. You will feel a profound impact in your life as well as at your Soul level.

However, no matter what information or advice you receive from the Akashic Records, you are the ultimate authority in your life and fully responsible for any and all actions you are taking.

Part I

Getting Ready for This Class

Those wise ones who see that the consciousness within them is the same consciousness within all beings, attain peace.
-THE KATHA UPANISHAD

Meditation

Let's start with a meditation that will help you relax and be at peace. This meditation is inspired by Dr. Joe Dispenza and has been adapted for the purpose of this exercise. Once you are finished with this meditation, move on to the exercise. You can record these instructions in your own voice or ask someone you trust to read them to you while you meditate. Go slowly.

Sit up straight with your feet flat on the floor. Let your hands rest on your knees. Make sure you keep your spine straight. Take a few very deep and very slow breaths. As you draw air into your nose, imagine that you are drawing in energy from the base of your spine and moving it all the way to the top of your head. Allow your energy to follow your awareness, and let your breath be your intention to relax and let go as you separate your mind from your body.

Do it one more time. Take your time. There is no rush. You have nowhere else to be. Just enjoy this moment and take one very slow and very deep breath. Inhale through your nose. Draw in energy from the base of your spine and allow it to travel all the way to the top of your head. Hold it on the top of your head with the intention of separating your mind from your body. Keep holding the energy on the top of your head. Then exhale and relax.

Take another very deep and very slow breath in through your nose. As you inhale, imagine you are drawing fluid up a straw and pull the energy through your body all the way up to your brain. Hold it on the top of your head. Let this energy follow your awareness and your breath to the top of your head and hold it there. As you exhale relax and let go of everything that's still lingering in your mind.

Do it one last time. Take a very deep and very slow breath. As you inhale through your nose, draw energy into your body, up your spine, and all the way to your brain. Hold it on the top of your head with the intention of pulling the mind out of the body.

Now pull the energy even higher until it is leaving your body and dissolving into the atmosphere. It is safe for you to do this. You are only letting go of your egocentric thoughts. You are releasing anything that doesn't serve you and has blocked your path. As you exhale you can feel deep relaxation and peace flowing through your mind and body. You are free. You are free and totally relaxed. You are free and at peace. All is well.

Now slowly regain your awareness, stretch your body, and open your eyes. After you bring your energy back into your body and become fully conscious of your surroundings, continue with the next section in this book.

Exercise

Write down your answers to the following questions. There are no right or wrong answers. Just write down whatever comes to your mind. We will work with these answers toward the end of this book. However, it is important for you to answer these questions before you continue with the lesson in order to prove that you are accessing your Akashic Records. You have to follow these guidelines thoroughly to make it happen.

1) What is most important for me to know at this time in my life?

2) Describe what unconditional love feels like to you.

What Does Akasha Mean?

You can search throughout the entire universe for someone who is more deserving of your love and affection than you are yourself,
and that person is not to be found anywhere.
You yourself, as much as anybody in the entire universe deserve your love and affection.
-BUDDHA

What Is the Meaning of Akasha?

First of all let me clarify that the Akashic Records (AR) are not part of one specific religion. The AR are mentioned in many religions' scriptures, such as Hinduism, Buddhism, Christianity, Judaism, Theosophy, and modern Paganism. This proves that the AR are a spiritual medium that crosses religious boundaries.

Akasha is a Sanskrit word meaning *the aether*, which includes all elemental (material) and metaphysical (nonmaterial) senses.[1]

What Does that Mean for Us?

The energy and essence of everything is included in the field of the Akashic Records. Material things are things with form like human beings, books, trees, and even money. Nonmaterial things include our thoughts, emotions, energies, vibration, and creations as well as the energy of all material things. In other words, everything is contained in the field of the Akashic Records. Nothing gets lost or overlooked. This field of the Akashic Records is the basis and essence of all things.

You Are Going to Learn to Speak a New Language

Ervin Laszlo says, "Like atoms, Akasha is indivisible, eternal, and unperceivable; but, unlike them, it is infinite and all-pervading. Akasha is inferred from the sensed quality of sound."[2]

What Does this Mean for You Taking This Class?

Sound is a vibration, and you are going to communicate with your AR through vibration. For example, imagine that you are sitting with ten people in one room. Each of you speaks a different language in addition to English. You can all hear a dog barking outside of the room. You can't see the dog, but you can hear it barking because the dog's vocal chords are emitting vibrations. You pick up the vibrations with the membranes in your ears. Your ears pass these vibrations on to your brain. Your brain comprehends what this vibration means according to its programming or past experiences. It then translates the sound for you into a language you will understand. All ten people in the room will pick up the same vibrations, but each person will translate them into different words depending on the language he or she speaks.

You will learn a new language during this class. You will learn how to pick up a vibration, in this case not with your ears but through your eighth chakra[3], and translate this vibration into something you can understand and work with.

Akasha Is the Essence, the Spirit, of All that Is Life

The universe is wider than our views of it.
-HENRY DAVID THOREAU

Modern Pagans[4] believe that Akasha, or spirit, is the fifth element, a spiritual force that the other four elements—earth, fire, air, and water—descend from. Some practitioners also believe that the combination of these four elements make up that which is Akasha and that Akasha is present in every living creature in existence; without Akasha, there is no spirit and no soul.

What Does this Mean for You Taking This Class?

We can imagine the Akashic Records as a huge container that holds everything. It is the matrix[5] that provides a foundation or the structure that allows everything else to exist. Ervin Laszlo, author of *Science and the Akashic Field*, concludes that the "quantum vacuum" is the fundamental energy- and information-carrying field that informs not just the current universe but all universes past and present. Laszlo describes how such an informational field can explain why our universe is so improbably fine-tuned as to form galaxies and conscious life forms, and why evolution is an informed, not random, process: "These wave packets, also called the A-Field, don't only store information occurring in the present moment, they contain all information, every thought, every deed, every development that has ever happened since this universe's existence. The Akashic Records are the enduring record of all that happens, and has ever happened, in space and time."

A Field of Information Between the Spaces of Particles!

The Akashic Records are the matrix[6], or web, that keeps everything together and creates oneness where the appearance of separation is present. Think of it as a spider web that connects everything with each other. This field, reaches everywhere. It is flexible. Depending on the particular object, it can be dense or light and yielding. It moves, adjusts, and reacts to specific information and vibrations it receives from its environment.

Akashic energy exists in all of us—in all that is alive. Because of our interconnectedness with all of life, we are able to tap into the realm of the AR and retrieve information about any given subject.

We are tapping into the essence of life.

Akasha and Past Lives

To be able to look back upon one's past life with satisfaction is to live twice.
-LORD ACTON

Akasha is also significant to the principle of karma and it acts as a storage medium for past lives.

Anthroposophy[7] speaks of the reincarnation of the human spirit. It states that human beings pass between stages of existence: incarnating into an earthly body, living on earth, leaving the body behind, and entering the spiritual worlds before returning to be born again into a new life on earth. After the death of the physical body, the human spirit reviews its past life, perceiving its events as they were experienced by the objects of its actions.

A complex transformation takes place between the review of the past life and the preparation for the next life. The individual's karmic condition eventually leads to a choice of parents, physical body, disposition, and capacities that provide the challenges and opportunities the soul needs for further development, which includes karmically chosen tasks for the future life.

What Does this Mean for You Taking This Class?

It means that we are working with the belief that reincarnation and past lives exist and may contain valuable data for our life's purpose and us.

On a more personal note, I have to admit that I didn't fully believe in the concept of past lives until I had been working with the Akashic Records for over a year. The ideas of karma and past lives didn't appeal to me or resonate with my Catholic upbringing. This changed drastically when my Akashic Records addressed my dinnertime eating habits. I asked a question about my lack of appetite in the evenings, and the Akashic Records told me that it is related to one of my past lives. During that lifetime the children were put to bed very early because my "former" parents didn't have any food to feed us. Being put to bed early spared our parents the pain of not being able to feed us. A shiver came over me when I received this answer because deep in my heart I knew that it was true. This explained my lack of an appetite at night and why I love to go to sleep early.

I've had many of these aha moments since then and have no problem talking about past lives. A lot of healing can come from uncovering the hidden origins of our habits, patterns, and beliefs.

Attributes of the Heart

A balanced and open heart chakra is the foundation of a joyful, happy and healthy life. A loving and open heart enables us to give and receive unconditional love, feel compassion, express gratitude and appreciation, and be forgiving. Our hearts and heart chakras are located in the center of our beings and control the flow of our energy between the body and the spirit. They also determine our health, strength, and balance on our physical, emotional, and spiritual levels.

What Does this Mean for You Taking This Class?

I have observed two things over the years while teaching this class. The first thing is that the student who

---

19

already lives a heart-centered life will connect with the Akashic Records in a serene and effortless manner. The second thing is that the student who lives a more mind-based life will have a huge "heart opening" during these first experiences.

I myself belonged to the second group. The first few times I opened my Akashic Records, I had heart—opening experiences: I immediately realized that all the things that had been worrying me were not important to my existence, purpose, and overall well-being. The only thing that truly mattered in life was love.

Today, because of a global awakening, more and more students belong to the first group that already lives a more heart-centered life. However, if you presently belong to the second group, you should be excited because you will experience a life-changing shift that words cannot describe.

The Pathway Prayer

Prayer is not asking. It is a longing of the soul.
-MAHATMA GANDHI

Making a connection to your Akashic Records is intentional. You need to be able to raise your energy to the level of your eighth chakra and hold your vibration at this level for the duration of the communication.

What Does this Mean for You Taking This Class?

This actually sounds more difficult than it is. You make conscious choices many times during your day. Picking up your phone to talk to a friend, preparing a meal to nourish your body, and watching TV to relax are just a few examples of how you do things intentionally.

During the process of connecting with your AR, you might intend to receive guidance and answers to assist you on your journey through life. Some of you have the intention to find more peace or to connect to your soul's purpose. It doesn't really matter what your intentions are as long as they are genuine and conscious, meaning you are aware of them.

The pathway prayer will assist you in aligning your energy to the vibration of your Akashic Records. The prayer is also designed to block out your ego so you can make the connection with your Akashic Records through your eighth chakra. The prayer will enable you to access your own Akashic Records anywhere and at any given time without any additional preparations or mystic rituals. It is simple and very easy to use.

At first the following story didn't have a lot of meaning for me. Even though I included the story of Johnny Prochaska in my classes' curriculum, I never really knew how much truth it held. In 2003 one of my students mentioned that she had taken an Akashic Records class during the early seventies in Dallas, Texas, and the teacher was Johnny Prochaska. I was immediately interested when she told me that she was one of his first students and still had all of the early class materials, which had been written by Prochaska himself.

This encounter helped me accept the mystical part of this story and allowed me to embrace the full spectrum of this teaching: to trust and to have an open heart and mind.

The history of the prayer begins in Mexico City with a man named Johnny Prochaska, an accountant living in Texas. While traveling for work in Mexico City, he had an unexpected encounter. While he was out walking one day, he saw a woman standing in a doorway. She had the face of an ancient Mayan who had called to him in his dreams for more than three years. When he entered her hut, she said to him, "So! At last you come." She told him of her people, the "Old Ones," who brought "the knowledge of time," which we now refer to as the Akashic Records, to Earth from the distant star pattern of Pleiades. When the Mayan civilization's time on Earth ended, there were a few individuals left behind who still held the key to accessing these precious records and keeping the knowledge pure and sacred.

Prochaska was taken to an ancient temple, where he made the decision to dedicate his life to the Akashic Records. He was given the sacred prayer in a ceremony where he was chosen to teach the use of the sacred prayer, which would open the records and awaken everyone who sought this knowledge.

The prayer we use today was translated from Mayan to Spanish and then to English and German. Prochaska returned to the United States in the sixties and began teaching others how to access the Akashic Records, both for themselves and others."

Science and the Akashic Field

As a man who has devoted his whole life to the most clear-headed science, to the study of matter, I can tell you as a result of my research about atoms this much: There is no matter as such.
All matter originates and exists only by virtue of a force, which brings the particle of an atom to vibration and holds this most minute solar system of the atom together. We must assume behind this force the existence of a conscious and intelligent mind.
-MAX PLANCK

Can Science Prove that the Field of the Akashic Records Exists?

Albert Einstein tried to find scientific prove for the existence of a "unified field". He believed that a space exists between the smallest particles and atoms, and he called this space the four-dimensional space-time continuum. Unfortunately, he never got to finish his research, but he said, "I just want to know God's thoughts. The rest are details."

Today scientists know that the space between the smallest particles of our universe is not empty. This space is a web or interconnecting field of information that interweaves every atom. It exists everywhere. It is one field of information that connects everything: the Akashic Field. This field is the collective memory of the universe and continuously interacts with matter at all levels. Everything that exists comes from this quantum field, which is the source and foundation for all things that inhabit our physical reality.

Ervin Laszlo says in his book *Science and the Akashic Field*, "Although it appears solid, in the last count matter is energy bound in quantized wave-packets, and these packets are further bound together to create the vast and harmonious architecture that makes up the world. However, these wave packets, also called the A-Field, don't only store information occurring in the present moment, they contain all information, every thought, every deed, every development that has ever happened since this universe's existence. The Akashic Record is the enduring record of all that happens, and has ever happened, in space and time. A field of information between the spaces of particles!"

Gregg Braden talks about this field that permeates all of creation in his book, *Awakening the Power of a Modern*

God: "Between 1993 and 2000, scientists documented evidence of a field of energy, which is described in three ways. The field is everywhere all of the time. The field exists from the very beginning, what we call the big bang in the theories of physics. The field has an intelligence; it responds to very specific qualities of human emotions. This field is now recognized as a conduit. It is this field that carries everything we hold within into the world beyond our bodies."

What Does this Mean for You Taking This Class?

It means that accessing the Akashic Records is not part of or dependent on a belief system. Rather, it is a skill you can acquire. It doesn't matter if you understand exactly how it works as long as you are willing to learn the skill. Just like we all live under the influence of the law of gravity even if we don't understand how it works, we all have the ability and birthright to connect to our own Akashic Records without needing to understand the scientific details.

Future Information in the Akashic Records

The distinction between the past, present and future is only a stubbornly persistent illusion.
-ALBERT EINSTEIN

Are the Akashic Records Useful in Predicting the Future?

The Akashic Records are a medium for consciousness development. They assist us in expressing our soul purpose rather than dwelling on our mundane, everyday experiences. From the perspective of the Akashic Records, it doesn't really matter whether we choose to get a degree or work as a clerk. What truly matters is who we are becoming relative to that choice. Our Akashic Records can help us make the best choices for everyone regarding a relationship, the challenges of a work environment, or any other subject. However, no future is written in stone. There will always be free will, lending an element of mystery to life.

Whenever I address my records regarding future events or goals, I like to ask my questions "backwards." For example, let's say I want to host a successful professional event two months from today. I would formulate my question as follows: "What do I need to know now to have a successful event two months from today?" Another question I could ask is, "Is there anything I need to let go of to be fully aligned with hosting a successful event?"

Framing questions in this manner takes our personal power out of the future, where we really don't have any power, and into the present, where all of our power exists. We also accept responsibility for our power so that we can co-create the desired outcome instead of expecting an outside force to take care of everything. Learning how to access your Akashic Records is all about being in the now and taking on the responsibility for your own power in order to create and manifest your reality.

Future Potentiality

Any future predictions that the Akashic Records give you are based on the energetic vibration you have when you ask a question. If your energy shifts, the potential future outcome will shift accordingly. Shift, in this case, can refer to gaining insight regarding the subject, being able to let go of resentment, experiencing a healing, or sometimes just being able to surrender and find faith again. Our work in the Akashic Records is meant to create a healing shift in your being. Therefore, our future will always be an improvement over our past.

Let me explain it to you a different way. Imagine this universe as a big mirror that reflects everything back to you exactly the way you give it out. If your energy is angry and carries resentment, it will present you with more experiences that create anger and resentment. Once you have a healing shift in your energy, the mirror of our universe will reflect the new image back to you, creating a better and more joyful future for yourself.

Clients often contact me to confirm that the house they just bought looks exactly like the house described to them during an Akashic Records consultation or that the person he or she just married is exactly like the one predicted during his or her reading. Others got the year-end bonus as promised by their Masters and Teachers. I believe that all of these clients experienced a healing shift during their AR reading. With this shift they let go of their fears and negative patterns, which created space for the "future potential" to manifest itself in their lives.

Who Is Present in the Akashic Records?

For beautiful eyes, look for the good in others;
for beautiful lips, speak only words of kindness; and for poise,
walk with the knowledge that you are never alone.
-AUDREY HEPBURN

When we access our Akashic Records we address our intentions to our Masters, Teachers, and Loved Ones.

The "Masters and Teachers" are beings with a very high and pure vibrational energy. They are not limited by a specific religion or our planetary system. They embody a very high and clear vibration. Some of them have incarnated in human form before, such as Jesus, Mother Mary, Sai Baba, and Buddha. Others, like Angels and Archangels, join from a different sphere. In general, the Masters and Teachers communicate with us as one unified energy instead of appearing solely as Jesus or an Angel.

I have never had only one Master deliver a message to me mainly because I am totally open and trusting toward any divine source and am not attached to the earthly form of our Teachers but rather appreciate their divine energy. For example, I had Mother Mary, Jesus, and Sai Baba step forward to communicate with a client during a reading. It wasn't that this individual Master had a special message for the client that could only be delivered by this particular Teacher, but rather that this particular Master had a very special meaning to the client. The client felt connected to the energy of this specific Teacher and experienced trust and a heart-opening feeling when this connection occurred.

The "Loved Ones" refer to our ancestors. The Akashic Records provide us with the opportunity to communicate with our Loved Ones once they have transformed and evolved to a different vibrational level. They love to talk to us, clarify the misunderstandings we carry with us, and assist us in our struggles with life because they have left behind the limited perception that confines human beings.

We will work on shifting our energy by revealing and eliminating the roots of an issue or a challenge so that we can achieve healing on all levels and create a harmonious life for ourselves and others. Our Loved Ones can be very helpful in assisting us to forgive old grudges and release resentments and old hurts so we can live our lives more peacefully and harmoniously with each other.

The Lords of the Akashic Records

The Lords of the Akashic Records are the Records' gatekeepers. They are the "security guards" who decide if someone is allowed to enter the Akashic Records and what kind of information will be revealed. They are the protectors of the Akashic Field and evaluate whether or not we meet all the requirements for access and if our intentions are genuine.

I had never doubted the importance of the Lords of the Akashic Records, but I had also never really valued their service either. This changed when I met a lady from Sedona, Arizona, who had been successfully accessing the Akashic Records in her own unique way for several decades. As we got to know each other and chitchatted about our experiences with the Akashic Records, she mentioned that she never really minds waiting outside the gate for the Lords to bring her the requested information. I was stunned. I had seen the gate in the process of opening my AR many times before, but I never had to wait in front of it. She was very surprised when I told her that I always talked to the Masters and Teachers directly. It had never occurred to her that this was even a possibility. I felt a sudden surge of love and appreciation flowing through me and thanked the Lords of the Akashic Records profoundly for always granting me access to the Masters and Teachers directly.

Being Grounded During Your Spiritual Work

Going home and spending time with your family
and your real friends
keeps you grounded.
-JENNIFER ELLISON

Being grounded is all about being aware of the physical while connecting to the spiritual.

How to Be Grounded When You Access Your Akashic Records

To be grounded while accessing your own Akashic Records, you should sit upright in a chair. Do not sit in the lotus position or on the floor. Most people do not find it helpful to access their AR while sitting in the lotus position.

Keep both feet flat on the ground.

Keep both eyes open while accessing your Akashic Records. Closing your eyes can easily get you lost in the strong energy and diminish your intentions and focus.

Look up when you access your Akashic Records. The energy of the Masters and Teachers is not found on the floor or under the table. Focus your attention upward, above you, toward a quiet spot on the wall or ceiling.

Why Is It So Important to Be Grounded?

A grounded person has balance and stability in his or her physical and emotional being. It enables him or her to function successfully in the five-sensory world. It also supports his or her innate healing abilities in the physical and spiritual realm. A grounded person feels more peaceful about life and has a healthy flow of energy in all chakras. Being properly grounded allows us to attain higher spiritual levels, such as the Akashic Records.

How Do You Know when You Are Not Grounded?

If you are not grounded, you might feel tense, fidgety, off balance, easily distracted, scattered, and unreal. You usually have either too much or too little energy and like to hold on to problems and emotions.

Grounding Techniques

Here are some ways to help ground yourself:
Eating healthy, natural food
Drinking water
Walking, especially in nature
Practicing sports, yoga, tai chi, et cetera
Gardening
Walking barefoot
Singing

Practically anything that balances your first and second chakras will keep you grounded.

Part II

Guidelines for Opening Your Own Akashic Records

A person should first be changed by a teacher's instructions, and guided by principles of ritual.
-Xun Zi

The following guidelines will support you in successfully accessing your own Akashic Records by providing you with the necessary foundation.

• Keep eye closing to a minimum. We are operating with a fully conscious mind so use care when choosing a location to open your records.

Keeping your eyes open as much as possible will help you maintain your focus on your Masters and Teachers. It will give you a stronger connection and help you stay grounded during this work. In the beginning, choose a quiet and peaceful place to connect with your Akashic Records. Once you are more experienced, you will be able to open your Akashic Records anywhere and at any time. It's like weight lifting in that you start out small and easy, and as you get stronger, you can safely expose yourself to more difficult tasks.

• Do not drive a car with your Akashic Records open.

Please be aware and respectful of your surroundings and environment when you access your Akashic Records. It is not safe for you to drive a car with your AR open because the records influence your energy field and decrease your reaction time.

• The Prayer is sacred.

This Prayer is dedicated to assisting you in integrating your divinity into your life. Please treat it respectfully and sincerely, and hold it with appreciation and gratitude in your heart.

• Do not consume *any* recreational drugs or alcohol twenty-four hours before opening your Akashic Records. Prescription medications are acceptable.

Drugs and alcohol do affect your energy field. The use of drugs and alcohol will make it very challenging for you to raise your energy to the level of your eighth chakra, where you make your connection with the Akashic Records.

• Use your full legal name to open your Akashic Records.

Use the full legal name you have today. Generally that's the name on your driver's license. Your name and the Pathway Prayer together will grant you access to your Akashic Records.

• Always *read* the Prayer to open your Akashic Records.

One purpose of the Pathway Prayer is to bypass the ego. Your brain works differently when you read something than when you recall something from memory. Reading the Prayer helps you make the connection from the physical to the metaphysical realm. In addition, it will help you become grounded while you are raising your energy to access your Akashic Records.

• Use good judgment when deciding how long to stay in the records. One must build up a tolerance to this energy.

During the first few exercises, stay in your Akashic Records as long as you feel comfortable. In other words, you will get the best results and communication if you end your session before you get tired. Over the years I have noticed that students tend to doubt the messages they received when they overextend their visits. Once you are used to the energy, you can go into the records for as long as you wish. So please be mindful of your own energy.

• Ground yourself after each time you have been in the Records.

To be grounded is all about being aware of your physical being while you are connecting with your spiritual side. Refer to the previous chapter for information on grounding techniques.

• Respond to all information and all experiences while your records are open.

Let go of all expectations and ideas you have about the question you are planning to ask in the Akashic Records. Have an open mind and heart and be willing to work with whatever you will receive as a response to your inquiry.

Many times you will have no idea where they are going with the answer you receive. You will have to follow this guidance blindly until the full message reveals itself to you as the reading evolves.

Let me give you an example of what blindly following guidance really means. During a practice session in which several students gave a reading to one client, the client asked the following question: "How can I help my middle son?" None of the students knew the client and her story. The client had triplets and all three boys were severely physically and mentally handicapped. I purposely stood back from the reading to observe my students and the client. The students were clearly struggling to answer the question because they were trying to understand what their Masters and Teachers were telling them. Finally the Akashic Records asked me to assist the students. As I turned to the students, the records said, "Repeat after us! Don't try to understand what the Masters and Teachers are telling you right now. Just tell your client exactly what you hear in the records. If we are telling you that all trees are red and have purple leaves with white stripes on them, that's exactly the way you are going to repeat it to your client." After hearing this, the students immediately opened up to the client and gave her the most wonderful messages and advice possible regarding her sons. They mastered the gift of trust and learned how to blindly follow guidance.

I've also noticed many times that grammar and spelling are not very important to the Masters and Teachers. Your messages are all about creating a vibrational shift within you. So don't be hard on yourself if your language skills are imperfect.

Part III

The Akashic Record Prayer

How to Use the Prayer

The Akashic Record Prayer

I ask God if He will have his Shield of Love and Truth around <u>me</u> permanently, so only God's Love and Truth will exist between you and me.

I allow the Masters, Teachers, and Loved Ones of <u>me</u> to channel through me, out of whatever realm, to say whatever they wish.

Directions for Opening the Akashic Records Prayer

To access your own Akashic Records, say the entire prayer aloud as written. Next, repeat it twice silently, using your first and last legal name where "me" is underlined.

Example:

1. Read out loud exactly as written:

I ask God if He will have his Shield of Love and Truth
around <u>me</u> permanently,
so only God's Love and Truth will exist between you
and me.

I allow the Masters, Teachers, and Loved Ones of <u>me</u>
to channel through me, out of whatever realm, to say
whatever they wish.

**2. Read silently and exchange the underlined "<u>me</u>"
with your legal name.**

I ask God if He will have his Shield of Love and
Truth around <u>me</u> (exchange with your legal name)
permanently, so only God's Love and Truth will exist
between you and me.

I allow the Masters, Teachers, and Loved Ones of <u>me</u>
(exchange with your legal name) to channel through
me, out of whatever realm, to say whatever they wish.

**3. Read silently and exchange the underlined "<u>me</u>"
with your legal name.**

I ask God if He will have his Shield of Love and
Truth around <u>me</u> (exchange with your legal name)

permanently, so only God's Love and Truth will exist
between you and me.
I allow the Masters, Teachers, and Loved Ones of
<u>me</u> (exchange with your legal name) to channel
through me, out of whatever realm, to say whatever
they wish.

In other words, you will use your name four times and
it will never be spoken out loud!

Cut this page out of the book so you can always have it at hand when you open your Akashic Records.

I ask God
if He will have his Shield
of Love and Truth
around <u>me</u> permanently,
so only God's Love and Truth
will exist between you and me.

I allow the Masters, Teachers,
and Loved Ones of <u>me</u>
to channel through me,
out of whatever realm,
to say whatever they wish.

Directions for Closing the Akashic Records for Oneself

Thank you, I love you.
-GABRIELLE ORR

You close your Akashic Records by thanking your Masters, Teachers, and Loved Ones for their information and saying aloud, "Amen, Amen, Amen," until you can sense that they are closed.

I am using a less traditional way to close my Akashic Records. After receiving permission from my Masters and Teachers, I now close my Records by saying, "I love you, thank you, thank you, thank you,", which resonates much more with me than the traditional way.

For the following exercises, please keep a pen and paper handy. I encourage you to write down your answers to your questions because you will not be able to remember everything that you receive from your Masters and Teachers, and I would like for you to be able to see that the answers you are receiving are really coming from your Akashic Records. So please answer all exercises in writing.

Don't jump ahead in the book. Follow the book page by page and trust that this process has been designed with divine intentions. No short cuts, please. Trust the process. You deserve to receive this gift, and I am dedicated to presenting it to you.

During the first few exercises, your energy will align from wherever it currently is in your body to the vibration of your eighth chakra. In the eighth chakra, you will make your connection with your Masters and Teachers in your Akashic Records. Since everybody has their energy on a very unique level, it is impossible for us to compare ourselves with others. This is truly an individual journey for each human being, so be kind, gentle, and patient with yourself and enjoy the evolutionary process.

Please do the first three exercises in one sitting so your energy is more contained and focused.

Part IV

Exercise 1

I want to know God's thoughts;
The rest are details.
-ALBERT EINSTEIN

This first Exercise is a gentle way to invoke the Akashic energy in your life.

Step 1
Open Your Akashic Records with the Prayer

Step 2
Take about five to ten minutes for this exercise.

Pay attention to any sensations you might experience in your body. Can you feel a warm sensation or tingling in your body?

Do you hear voices?

Are you seeing images?

How do you feel emotionally?

Gently pay attention to whatever you are experiencing. Don't try too hard or try to force something to happen.

Step 3
Write down your experiences.

Step 4
Close your Akashic Records.

Exercise 2

*We keep moving forward, opening new doors,
and doing new things, because we're curious and curiosity
keeps leading us down new paths.*
-WALT DISNEY

Step 1
Open Your Akashic Records with the Prayer

Step 2
Ask the following questions:

Are my Akashic Records open?
Masters and Teachers, can you please give me a sign
that I am in my Akashic Records?

Step 3
Write down your experiences.

Write down anything that is going through your mind right now. Remember not to judge it for its content or source. Just follow the flow of what you are experiencing and write down what comes to your mind.

Pay attention to any sensations you might experience in your body. Do you feel more energy in your head, neck, and shoulder area? To me it feels like someone is pushing a cotton-candy pillow down on my head. It feels light and heavy at the same time but never uncomfortable.

Do you hear a voice or voices?

Are you seeing images?

How do you feel emotionally?

Please remember to write everything down while your Akashic Records are open.

Step 4
Close your Akashic Records.

Exercise 3

*Your task is not to seek for love, but merely
to seek and find
all of the barriers within yourself that you
have built against it.*
-A Course in Miracles

Step 1
Open Your Akashic Records with the Prayer

Step 2
Ask the following questions:

Are my Akashic Records open?
Masters and Teachers, what is most important for me
to know at this time in my life?

Step 3
Write down your experiences.

Like in the previous exercise, write down anything that is going through your mind right now. Remember not to judge it for its content or source. Just follow the flow of what is happening and write down what comes to your mind.

Breathe in and out through your heart chakra.

Pay attention to any sensations you might experience in your body. Do you feel more energy in your head, neck, and shoulder area? To me it feels like someone is pushing a cotton-candy pillow down on my head. It feels light and heavy at the same time but never uncomfortable.

Do you hear a voice or voices?

Are you seeing images?

How do you feel emotionally?

Please remember to write everything down while your Akashic Records are open.

Step 4
Close your Akashic Records.

Once you've closed your Akashic Records, read the answers again and see if you can feel their energy. Then compare the answers you have just received and written down with the answers you wrote down for the very first exercise in this book. You will notice that it is exactly the same question. How has your answer changed? Can you notice a difference between the answer from the very first exercise and the answer now?

The first answer (from page 4) is *your* answer and the second answer (from just now) is the answer given to you by the Akashic Records.

Have the pronouns (I, me, you, we, et cetera) changed? The pronouns used in answer number one are usually "I" and "me." The pronouns used in answer number two are "you" and "we" because the Akashic Records are talking to you and giving you advice.

Has the quality of the answer changed?
Students usually write down questions in answer number one like "Am I on my life's path," "Where do I go from here," and "What is my soul's purpose?" In answer number two the student usually receives answers to the questions written down in answer number one. Please notice that both exercises are exactly the same. The only difference is that the second time around the student has his or her Akashic Records open.

Has the content of the answer changed? Answer number one is usually more worry- and fear-based whereas the message in answer number two is coming from love, guidance, and encouragement. This is a huge difference.

Has the formality and quality of the language changed? In answer number one, we write down our answers the way we usually talk. Don't be surprised if in answer number two the language is more sophisticated and formal.

Has the energy of the answer changed? Many students feel emotional when receiving answer number two but treat answer number one as a normal exercise and try to get it perfect.

.

Exercise 4

When words become unclear,
I shall focus with photographs.
When images become inadequate,
I shall be content with silence.
-ANSEL ADAMS

Working with Images

This exercise is designed to enable you to see images in your Akashic Records and teach you how to establish communication with your Masters and Teachers. Make sure you ask a lot of questions until you fully understand the meaning of the image you receive.

Envision yourself holding a remote control in your hand that lets you zoom in and out of the experience, ask for clarification, sharpen the image, add colors, or change the image to black and white.

Images are an important part of our communication with our Akashic Records. When we receive images during our communication with the Akashic Records, we need to make sure that we do not interpret these images ourselves. Instead we should ask our Masters and Teachers for the meaning of the images they show us.

For example, if you see a rose while in the AR, don't assume that it stands for romance but rather ask for the exact meaning of this image. The Masters and Teachers once showed me a rose for a female client, and she wanted to take it as a sign that her current partner was the perfect lover for her. The Masters and Teachers continued to explain that the rose had some very strong thorns for protection, which meant that her partner was not ready for the relationship she wanted to experience.

Step 1
Open up your Akashic Records with the prayer.

Step 2
Ask the following questions:

Are my Akashic Records open?
Masters and Teachers, what is the most important thing for me to know at this time in my life?
Please show me the answer in an image and explain the image to me.

For this exercise you might want to close your eyes for a little while. Many people can see images easier with their eyes closed, at least in the beginning. Stay with the image for a while until you have a real feeling for it and then write down your experiences.

Step 3
Write down anything that you see in the image. Go back and forth between looking at your image to writing down your experiences and keep on asking questions about the image until you are satisfied. Picture yourself looking at a painting and being able to ask the artist why he or she painted it this way and used these colors. Be like Sherlock Holmes and ask questions until you are clearly seeing the answer.

Breath in and out through your heart chakra, relax, and smile.

Step 4
Close your Akashic Records.

Once you've closed your Akashic Records, read the answer again and see if you can feel its energy. Most people see images easily and have no problems understanding the symbolic meaning of them, but please don't feel discouraged if you weren't able to see an image. You probably have more of an audible connection than visual strength.

In any case, the most important thing is to receive the energy. Images or words are secondary because it is the energetic vibration that will make a difference in your life.

How to Use this Exercise During Your Daily Practices

I enjoy working with images in my Akashic Records. They help me to receive an answer that feels totally unexpected and new to me, which is always a nice confirmation that the messages are coming from my Masters and Teachers and not from myself.

Here are some suggestions on how you can work with images in your Akashic Records.

• You can ask for images like smiley faces or a rating on a scale from one to ten to help you determine if something is in your highest interest or not.
Masters and Teachers, please show me a smiley-face image that will make clear to me if it is in my highest interest to choose _____.
Masters and Teachers, please show me on a scale from one to ten, with one being the worst and ten being the best, if _____ is in my highest interest.

• You can also start to establish your own signs and their meanings with your Records. This is beneficial if you receive an answer you feel insecure or doubtful about. You can then fall back on your own private "sign language" with the Akashic Records.
Masters and Teachers, please show me a sign that means yes, a sign that means no, one for going forward, and one for stopping.

For years I used a sunflower as a symbol for yes and a traffic stop sign as an indicator for no.

Exercise 5

*I do believe we're all connected. I do
believe in positive energy.*
-HARVEY FIERSTEIN

Feeling the Energy of the Akashic Records

Some things are impossible to explain with words.
Words can only take you so far. They can serve as a
pointer to the destination but cannot be the destination. Some things just have to be felt. This exercise
will bring you closer to feeling the vibration of your
Akashic Records while you receive their guidance.
Feeling the vibration of the Akashic Records will allow
you to open up your heart and live your life in a peaceful and balanced way.

Step 1
Open your Akashic Records with the prayer.

Step 2
Ask the following questions:

Are my Akashic Records open?
Masters and Teachers, please let me feel what unconditional love feels like to you.

Close your eyes for a moment and allow yourself to just feel.

Step 3
Then write down your experiences as much as possible. As I already said, it is sometimes very difficult to put feelings into the proper wording.

Step 4
Close your Akashic Records.

I am always amazed by the answers my students receive when they do this exercise. Usually their heart chakras open. Their experiences are unexpected and hard to put into words. The feeling is bigger, more expansive, and grander than imagined and doesn't have much to do with the way we would describe love in general.

Go back to page 4 and compare the answer you have just received with the answer you wrote down back then. How do the answers differ from each other? Please remember that the answer from page 4 was *your* explanation of unconditional love and the answer from this exercise reflects the way your Akashic Records experience unconditional love. Usually the second answer is much more pure, heartfelt, and unlimited, whereas your answer is coming more from the intellect.

How to Use this Exercise during Your Daily Practices

You can ask to feel peace, love, joy, or excitement in your life. You can also ask what it would feel like to be healthy, wealthy, happy, loved, successful, or anything else you would like to experience in your life. For example, a lot of people would like to have more money in their lives. If this is on your wish list as well, you can ask the following questions:

Masters and Teachers, please let me feel what prosperity feels like to you.
How can I integrate this feeling into my life?

Another example of how to use this form of questions would be:

Masters and Teachers, please let me feel how loved I am.
Masters and Teachers, please let me feel what it feels like to be successful.

Exercise 6

To raise new questions, new possibilities,
to regard old problems
from a new angle, requires creative imagination.
-ALBERT EINSTEIN

How to Ask the Right Questions in Your Akashic Records

The questions you ask in the Akashic Records have a specific quality and vibration. The higher and clearer the vibration and intention is, the easier it will be for you to receive and understand the answers.

Form each question around a specific challenge or problem.

Good questions are clear even if they are broad.

Ask one main question about your challenge and then several subquestions to clarify the answer.

Questions that are asked in a "should" form are not very beneficial because it indicates an expectation as well as future manifestation from a point of view in the past. For example, should I go back to school to increase my income? Should I move to a different area to let go of my past? The Masters and Teachers will never force us to go in one specific direction. We will always have free will. Their guidance is loving, gentle, and kind.

The same is true for questions that are asked in a "would" form because they often express probability or presumption. For example, would it be good for me to move into a new area to be happier in my life? Would I be healthier if I wouldn't be in such a stressful relationship with my husband? Would I be successful if I would have gone to college?

Set your main question in the present. Some of the follow-up questions might take you into your past so you can eliminate the origin of a problem or into the future so you can create a new thought pattern or belief that benefits you more on your life's journey.

Be curious like a child and ask questions like in the title song of the German version of *Sesame Street*: "Who, how, what—why, why, and why—those who don't ask stay dumb." You can also think of yourself as a reporter and ask your questions until you are fully satisfied with the result.

Here Are Some Examples On How You Can Ask The Most Beneficial Questions During Your Daily Practices

- What is most important for me to know at this time in my life?
- What do I need to know to live in alignment with my soul purpose?
- What do I need to know to remember who I truly am and what I came here to do?
- What do I need to know to be fully present for this event/meeting/relationship/investment?
- Is there anything I need to let go of (judgment, fear, anxiety, prejudice) to be fully present for this event/meeting/relationship/investment?
- What do I need to know to receive clear and authentic answers from my Akashic Records?
- What is this situation teaching me?
- What is the deeper purpose of this experience and what do I need to learn from it?
- How can I let go of this problem or challenge?
- What do I need to know to experience balance and peace in my life?
- What do I need to know about being successful?
- What definition of success applies to me and how can I implement it into my life?
- What are the underlying reasons for my health challenges?
- What do I need to know to shift these underlying reasons and create health and well-being in my life?
- What is my purpose in my relationships and how can I align myself with this purpose?
- What do I need to know to live in alignment with my creator?
- How can I strengthen my relationship with my creator?

Exercise 7

Knowledge is love and light and vision.
-HELEN KELLER

Inquiring Information About Neutral Subjects

In this kind of exercise, a neutral subject refers to a subject that doesn't create an emotional reaction within you—something you are interested in or you relate to and is easy for you to observe with an indifferent attitude. It could pertain to your hobbies, work environment, social interests, scientific discoveries, and many other things.

Getting comfortable with this kind of exercise will help you have a deeper understanding of things, allow you to see situations from a different and neutral perspective, and gain valuable information about any subject in your everyday life.

I once asked to receive information regarding Harley Davidson motorcycles. The first thing the Masters and Teachers let me hear was the deep sound of a Harley's motor. Then they let me experience a strong feeling of pride, the wonderful feeling of belonging to a community, and being part of something special.

My records told me how the company started. They talked about the struggles the owners had to go through to make, and keep, this motorcycle special and unique. I was able to feel the excitement and determination of Mr. Harley and Mr. Davidson, and I will never look at these motorcycles the same way.

Another time I asked for information about massage therapy. The Akashic Records showed me how a thumb applies pressure to a muscle and how this touch eventually will reach every other cell in the body. The stimulation of the muscle tissue impacts the nervous system and therefore every other system in our bodies. Massage therapy reaches far beyond just treating our muscles. It is truly healing to our whole being.

Step 1
Open up your Akashic Records with the prayer.

Step 2
Think of a neutral subject you would like to receive some more information about.

Ask the following questions:

Are my Akashic Records open?
Masters and Teachers, please give me information about_____(fill in your neutral subject).

Close your eyes for a moment and allow yourself to just feel.

Step 3
Then write down your experiences as much as possible.

Step 4
Close your Akashic Records.

Did you gain any new insight? Maybe you received confirmation about your interest that will allow you to enjoy it even more. I usually am able to see things from a different perspective, which allows me to approach it in a more informed way.

How to Use this Exercise During Your Daily Practices

Use this exercise as often as possible. Ask about your hobbies, TV shows, food, diets, exercise programs, cars, yoga, meditation, books, real estate, pets, animals, plants, global warming, politics, and so on.

If you practice this exercise often, you will discover a whole new side of life and subsequently yourself.

Exercise 8

Our prime purpose in this life is to help others.
And if you can't help them, at least don't hurt them.
-DALAI LAMA

Inquiring Information Regarding Other People

Are we allowed to ask questions about other people in the Akashic Records? Absolutely, as long as the questions are in relationship to yourself. Theoretically, you can ask any question you like. If it doesn't pertain to you, you will not receive an answer. If the question isn't asked with integrity, you will either hear nothing or remarks like "Why do you ask? This is not for you to know! A better question for you to ask would be _____." Sometimes the records will turn the question around and make it about the person who is asking. For example, if you ask a question like "Are my coworkers talking about me behind my back?" the records' reply might be, "Why is it so important to you what others choose to do?"

In any case, please know that you will get the best results if you ask with the highest integrity and you make it about your own growth and journey. The following exercise will provide you with some good examples.

Before you open your records think of someone who annoys you.

Step 1
Open your Akashic Records with the prayer.

Step 2
Ask the following questions:

Are my Akashic Records open?
Masters and Teachers, what do I need to know about this person (who annoys me) in relationship to me?
Please show me this person through the eyes of the Akashic Records.
What do I need to know to improve/heal this relationship?
or
What do I need to know about this person to understand him or her or the situation?

Step 3
Answer one question after the other and write your experiences down.

Make sure you ask all four questions while you have your Akashic Records open and don't stop prematurely. The fourth question is really the most important question of this exercise.

Step 4
Close your Akashic Records.

Did you gain any new insights about this person and your relationship to him or her?

Are you able to feel that the Akashic Records do not pass judgment or feel prejudice toward this person?

The third question of this exercise allows you to get a feeling for the other person's struggle and pain, which will allow you to open your heart more and to let go of the many misperceptions and assumptions the ego holds. It's almost as if we get to walk for a few steps in the other person's shoes.

In any case, I have never experienced any judgment from the records toward any person, including myself. Unconditional love is really the only thing the Masters and Teachers generate.

How to Use this Exercise During Your Daily Practices

You can ask for information about anyone as long as it relates to you in some way. It doesn't have to be someone who annoys you. Ask about your parents, children, partner, coworkers, neighbors, friends, and family. You can also ask about a company, politicians, and other personalities.

Please remember that you will get the most out of your questions when you ask to see circumstances from the Akashic Records' perspective as well. Don't stay stuck and limited within your point of view. The following three questions provide a beneficial structure to keep you focused on your intentions so that you can create a healing shift.

Masters and Teachers, what do I need to know about this person in relationship to me?
Please show me this person through the eyes of the Akashic Records.
What do I have to know about this person to see this relationship from a broader perspective?

Exercise 9

All the world's a stage, and all the men
and women merely players:
they have their exits and their entrances;
and one man in his time plays many parts,
his acts being seven ages.
-WILLIAM SHAKESPEAR

Past Lives

At this point we have to ask ourselves if past lives exist. Did we experience a lifetime before this one, and did we have experiences that might still be affecting us today? I didn't believe in past lives when I started my journey with the Akashic Records. I flat-out denied their existence even though I didn't really know anything about them back then. The concept just felt creepy to me, and I didn't want anything to do with it.

Today I know that past lives do exist. During my work with the Akashic Records, I have experienced and felt it on every level and have no reason to feel uncomfortable around this subject anymore. My rule of thumb is that I am living now, and that's where I want to keep my energy. However, sometimes it is beneficial to revisit an experience from a past life in order to live a better life today. So I am embracing the opportunity to do so.

The following questions will guide you into a past life experience of your own. Please know that you have nothing to be afraid of. You are always in control and can only learn and benefit from this exercise.

Step 1
Open your Akashic Records with the prayer.

Step 2
Ask the following questions:

Are my Akashic Records open?
Masters and Teachers, show me a pattern I have today that originates from a past lifetime.

Please make sure that you let your Masters and Teachers pick a pattern of yours because you don't know if the pattern originates from a past life or not. Take your time, don't rush; the pattern will come.

How does this pattern relate to a past lifetime? Get a feeling for the past life the records are referring to. Can you understand what happened back then? Notice if you see in color or black and white. Can you smell something or hear voices or music? Are you aware of the environment you were in during this past life? Be sensitive to everything and know that you are always safe and in control. You can always turn to your Masters and Teachers for more guidance or comfort.

Ask for advice on how to shift the pattern.

Step 3
Write your experiences down as much as possible.

Step 4
Close your Akashic Records.

Did you gain any new insight?

Here is an example from my own experience. One pattern the records showed me during this exercise was that I love to have clean floors. Even though that is correct, I was very surprised. I thought that it was normal and never expected it to be a residual influence from a past life. My floors are always clean. I don't mind if the windows are dirty or if there is some dust on the bookshelves, but my floors are always clean. When I asked to see from where this pattern originates, they showed me that I was a small girl living and working in an old monastery. It was my job to clean the hallways whenever the nuns came in from the gardens or the city. If I did a good job, I received a full meal at night. If I didn't do a good job, I only received bread and water. Clean floors were essential to my survival, and so that pattern has stayed with me. When I asked how to shift this pattern, my Masters and Teachers told me that it wasn't a big deal. They said I should just be aware of it and not let it control my morning routine. My solution: I bought a Roomba, which is a self-propelled vacuum cleaner. Problem solved.

How to Use this Exercise During Your Daily Practices

At some point you will be working in your records on an issue of yours and your Masters and Teachers will tell you that it originates from a past lifetime. If that's the case, just follow up with questions three and four from this exercise to get more information about your inquiry.

You can also ask directly about past lives concerning people in your life or places you feel drawn to.

Is there a past life connection between this person and me?
Do I feel drawn to this place because of an experience from a past life?

Please make sure that the question relates to your present life because that's the experience your soul has chosen for this moment. I don't find it beneficial to ask random questions regarding past lives. Keep it real and stay focused and grounded in your integrity.

Exercise 10

The teacher who is indeed wise
does not bid you to enter the house of his wisdom
but rather leads you to the threshold of your mind.
-KHALIL GIBRAN

Prayers and Affirmations

Prayer is the invocation to connect with a divine energy through deliberate communication, either to express gratitude, to celebrate the joy of being alive, to seek guidance and advice, or to request help and support.

We will work with prayer in the Akashic Records by getting familiar with prayers that have been given to us through the records. We will also ask to receive prayers that are for our own unique purposes. The prayers can be used while you are in your Akashic Records or out of the records.

Prayers Received Through the Akashic Records

Prayer for Loved Ones and Entities

Father/Mother/God, we ask that this entity/soul be sent on in its spiritual evolution for the highest good and mutual benefit of everyone concerned.

This prayer is beneficial to say for anyone who has passed on. It doesn't matter if we personally knew the deceased or if he or she is a stranger. You can support anyone who is moving on into the other realm by saying this prayer.

This prayer also helps with clearing spaces of stuck energy, a practice that is often used in Feng Shui or in other rituals by smudging with sage.

The prayer starts with Father/Mother/God so that we do not create a conceptual image of the divine creator but rather eliminate our ego's need to control our reality.

Prayer for Releasing Outside Influences

*If what I am experiencing is not mine, may God
have his shield around me,
and I release whatever it may be to him.*

This prayer helps to clear ourselves of thoughts
and emotions that are not linked to our own being
and experiences. Sometimes people who work very
intensely with others are prone to take on others' pains
and problems. They are very empathetic, and they can
lose sight of what their own energy is and what belongs
to the other person. Nurses, massage therapists, and
other body workers often carry their clients' problems
without really being aware of it. This prayer is a wonderful way to clear your energy from any interference.

Prayer for Forgiveness of Yourself and Others

*If there is anyone or anything that has hurt me in the
past, knowingly or unknowingly,
I forgive and release it.*

*If I have hurt anyone or anything in the past,
knowingly or unknowingly,
I forgive and release it.*

Forgiveness is the renunciation of resentment, anger, and bitterness as a result of a perceived offense, disagreement, assault, or mistake. Forgiveness is also another word for "letting go of something." When someone practices forgiveness, he or she is letting go of the resentment, anger, and bitterness he or she is holding in his or her own energy field. Replacing these energies with love, understanding, and peace has a tremendous effect on us in every area of our lives. Forgiveness will set "you" free!

This prayer serves double duty by allowing us to forgive others as well as asking others to forgive us. It is not necessary to address every incident or person specifically. The intention and willingness to forgive and to ask to be forgiven will be the most important components. The rest is up to the universe.

Affirmations

Affirmations are meant to give you a different, more positive, and constructive perspective of your problem than you currently have. We work with them in the records in the same way we work with prayers.

For this exercise think of a problem you have in your life currently.

Step 1
Open up your Akashic Records with the prayer.

Step 2
Ask the following questions:

Are my Akashic Records open?
Masters and Teachers, please give me a prayer or affirmation that will help me with my current problem.

Ask for instructions on how often to recite the prayer or affirmation.

Step 3
Write your experiences down as much as possible.

Step 4
Close your Akashic Records.

Did you receive a prayer or affirmation that helped you shift your perspective of your current problem?

Here is an example. A client asks to receive a prayer to have healthy self-esteem. The records give the client the following prayer/affirmation: "I am the center of the universe!" and instruct the client to recite these words whenever he starts to complain about others.

A different client asks to receive a prayer that will help her write a book. Here is the answer she received:
"It's like giving birth.
"First you conceive;
"Then you deliver;
"Then you nurture;

"And then you have to let it go to give birth to another creation."

How to Use this Exercise During Your Daily Practices

These prayers and affirmations can act like a quick vitamin boost. As we become aware of our fears and negative patterns, we can fall back on the prayer we received from the Akashic Records to prevent us from losing energy or going deeper into our pain-body[8]. We can use these prayers like a mantra, repeating them over and over again in order to let go of our unwanted thoughts and issues. With time we will understand that "We truly are the center of the universe" and allow our creativity to flow freely.

You can ask for prayers regarding every area of your life, such as health, wealth, balance, peace, career, relationships, creations, and spirituality.

Exercise 11

*Happiness cannot be traveled to, owned,
earned, worn or consumed.
Happiness is the spiritual experience of living
every minute with love, grace, and gratitude.*
-DENIS WAITLEY

Grace Points

Grace Points are pressure points located in either of your hands. When gently touched, Grace Points stimulate the energy meridians in your body that are connected to your heart and soul being. Consciously using intention or prayer while holding these points allows you to relax, reconnect with divine wisdom, and move into an open, receptive state of clarity and peace.

Grace is the freely-given unconditional love and forgiveness of source that regenerates and strengthens human beings. Everybody has the ability to open up to

111

receive grace during times of difficulty. The only pre-requisites are that we must be receptive and in a state of gratitude.

The following Grace Points have been received through the Akashic Records (in conjunction with the Akashic Records Consultants International organization) and can be used on either of your hands while your Akashic Records are open or closed.

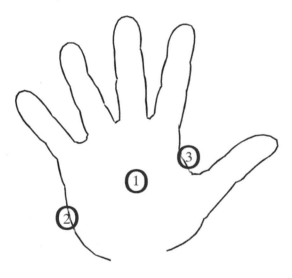

Point One: Main Grace Point,
located in the center of the palm
Applying pressure to this point helps you release any contracted energy you are holding so that you can see things more clearly. It also opens you up to more posi-tive and peaceful experiences in your life.

Point Two: Body Release Point,
located in the middle of the side of the palm under
your pinky
Stimulating the energy of this point allows you to
release stagnant energy like judgments, emotions,
pain, and negative beliefs and patterns from your
body.

Point Three: Ancestry Point,
located in the web between the thumb and index finger
Applying pressure to this point helps you release
judgments, beliefs, and emotions that have been
passed on through the DNA or through your genetic
lineage.

How to Use the Grace Points

Before you start working with the Grace Points, think
of an issue you would like to have clarified or let go of.

Set your intention to be at peace and experience divine
grace in your being.

Step 1
Open up your Akashic Records with the prayer.

Step 2
Ask the following questions:

Are my Akashic Records open?

Masters and Teachers, please support me in releasing the following issue for the highest good and mutual benefit of everyone concerned.

(Use the issue you previously chose before opening your Akashic Records.)
Masters and Teachers, please assist me in receiving grace and divine peace.

With the thumb of one hand, gently apply pressure to the Main Grace Point on the other hand. Focus all of your attention on applying pressure to this point and your issue at the same time. Take your time with this, three to four minutes or until you feel a shift in your energy.

Look at the picture with the hand to make sure you chose the correct Grace Point.

Please remember that applying pressure to this point helps you release any negative energy you are holding so that you can see things more clearly. It also opens you up to having more positive and peaceful experiences in your life.

With the thumb of one hand, gently apply pressure to the Body Release Point on the other hand. Focus all of your attention on applying pressure to this point and your issue at the same time. Take your time with this, three to four minutes or until you feel a shift in your energy.

Gabrielle Orr

Look at the picture with the hand to make sure you chose the correct Grace Point.

Please remember that applying pressure to this point allows you to release stagnant energy like judgments, negative beliefs, emotions, and pain from your body.

With the thumb of one hand, gently apply pressure to the Genetic Lineage Point on the other hand. Focus all of your attention on applying pressure to this point and your issue at the same time. Take your time with this, three to four minutes or until you feel a shifting of your energy.

Look at the picture with the hand to make sure you chose the correct Grace Point.

This point supports you in releasing judgments, beliefs, and emotions that have been passed down through the DNA or your genetic lineage.

Step 3
Write your experiences down.

Step 4
Close your Akashic Records.

I know this process sounds too easy to be effective. However, I have witnessed so many aha moments in my clients, students, and myself that I feel compelled to share these Grace Points with you. May they serve you as well as they have served me.

115

How to Use this Exercise During Your Daily Practices

Use the Grace Points whenever you feel one of your patterns emerging. It's a very simple tool, and you should be able to remember the points and sequence easily after a few practices.

It is also safe for you to use the Grace Points when you are not in your Akashic Records. You can practice the routine anytime you feel upset, anxious, or ready to let go of something. Divine support is always with you when your intentions are genuine and clear.

Exercise 12

True wisdom comes to each of us
when we realize how little we understand about life,
ourselves, and the world around us.
*-*SOCRATES

Contacting Ancestors

We are genetically related to someone if he or she is our ancestor or if we share a common ancestor. We all have ancestors — both of blood and of spirit — who can be sources of healing, guidance, and companionship. The ancestors we choose to honor may include recent and/or more distant family members. Our ancestors can offer us vital support via advice and insight as we fulfill our potential here on Earth. Part of our ancestors' post-death journey may include making amends for their wrong doings while here on Earth. For their sake as well as for ours, it's good to spend a little time cultivating our relationships with our ancestors in order to receive deeper insight into the origin of our patterns and issues.

Just because our Loved Ones are deceased doesn't mean that they are part of the Masters and Teachers in the Akashic Records. However, we can communicate with them by using our connection with our Masters and Teachers in the Akashic Records.

Step 1
Open up your Akashic Records with the prayer.

Step 2
Ask the following questions:

Are my Akashic Records open?
Masters and Teachers, please allow an ancestor of mine to step forward. (It is not unusual to have more than one ancestor show up for this exercise. They love to talk to us. If you have more than one ancestor who wants to connect with you, request that the one who is most beneficial for this exercise stay and continue the dialog with you.)

Ask for the ancestor to identify him- or herself. You want to know what kind of relationship you have with each other, like uncle, aunt, grandfather, great grandmother, et cetera.

Ask your ancestor to clarify a misperception that you acquired during your childhood.

For example:

You might be afraid of dogs because your mother always panicked when she saw a dog coming close to you or you might have abandonment issues because your parents separated during your childhood. It could also be that you experience low self-esteem because your parents didn't have enough money to buy you new clothes, which made you feel unworthy of nice and beautiful things.

Ask if you are still holding on to the event that has created the pattern or issue.

Do you still feel abandoned, have low self-esteem, or feel as if you don't deserve nice things?

Ask your ancestor to help you heal this event and let go of your misperceptions.

Masters and Teachers, what do I need to know to let go of this experience and feel at peace with it?

Step 3
Write your experiences down.

Step 4
Close your Akashic Records.

Were you able to recognize your ancestor?

What did the energy feel like?

Were you able to understand your ancestor's advice?

Our ancestors love to talk to us. Their main intent is for us to feel loved and cared for at all times. They also understand that most of our suffering derives from misunderstandings and misperceptions. Once you are able to see a situation from a different perspective, you will be able to let go of the undesirable beliefs you are holding on to and be at peace with the events of your past.

How to Use this Exercise During Your Daily Practices

Contact your ancestors whenever you feel that you have unresolved issues with an event from your past. You can ask for a specific ancestor, such as your Uncle Billy, or leave it up to the Akashic Records to have the right one for this situation come forward and talk to you.

It is possible that ancestors may just step forward during one of your exercises to talk to you without you requesting their presence. Please remember that you are in control of the reading and have the choice whether or not to communicate with an ancestor.

Exercise 13

It's the game of life. …
I gotta have as much fun and go around the board
as many times as I can
before it's my turn to leave.
-TUPAC SHAKUR

Oracle Cards, Angel Cards, Inspirational Quotes, Newspapers, and Other Tools

Sometimes I like to "play" with oracle and angel cards in my Akashic Records. These cards usually have a very positive outlook on life and are meant to guide you toward your higher purpose. I use these cards in my own unique way instead of how the author intended.

You could receive a response regarding an issue or problem that may seem totally unrelated to the original question. You might be surprised by an unpredicted answer that doesn't sound like your internal dialogs, which by now you are probably accustomed to. This is a very efficient way to cut your ego out of a reading and makes it very easy for you to receive a clear answer from your Akashic Records.

Step 1
Open up your Akashic Records with the prayer.

Step 2
Ask the following question:

Are my Akashic Records open?

Pick a card from a deck of your choice, read the card, and then ask your Masters and Teachers, "How does this card relate to me?" or, "How does this card relate to an issue of mine?"

Step 3
Write your results down.

Step 4
Close your Akashic Records.

Either question will provide you with answers that pertain to what you are experiencing in your life at this time.

How to Use this Exercise During Your Daily Practices

You can use any kind of cards, articles, books, or quotes for this exercise.

I like to use the "Power Thought Cards" by Louise L. Hay or the "Inner Peace Cards" by Dr. Wayne Dyer. But other cards work just as well. You can also just take a newspaper article or a paragraph from a book and ask your Akashic Records how this article or paragraph relates to you.

It doesn't matter which tool you choose for this exercise because your Masters and Teachers will provide you with the appropriate answer you need to hear in order to move forward with your situation.

Part V

Making the Akashic Records Practice Your Own

An ounce of practice is worth more than tons of preaching.
-Mahatma Gandhi

How Often Should I Access My Own Akashic Records?

As often as possible. This is not one of your cell phone plans where you have limited minutes. Your access is unlimited. Communicate with your Akashic Records daily. The more you practice your connection and communication, the more aligned you will be with this source. Once you feel comfortable with your Masters and Teachers, you can change your daily routine and make the connection when questions arise, even if this is only two or three times a week.

What Questions Do I Ask?

Ask any question that will help you with your life and your journey. Use the questions from this book and tailor them to your needs. Be kind to yourself even if you find yourself asking the same questions over and over again. You are on an evolutionary journey. Sometimes it takes us a while to move through a phase and experience progress in our lives. Give yourself the time and attention you need to move through your challenges and make this a happy and joyful experience.

Keep It Sacred

Keep this process sacred and divine. The Pathway Prayer is a unique process that works for anyone who resonates with its energy. Many times we feel excited about something and want to share it with others. My advice for you is to share your experiences with others but staying detached from their receptivity. If your friends are open to your offering, enjoy their response. If your friends don't show any interest or speak out against it, then honor where they are on their paths and enjoy their responses as well. It is far more important for you to stay focused on your own sacred experience than to mingle in someone else's business. Ultimately, whatever you do for yourself will affect everybody else. Whether you are aware of it or not, everything you do has a significant effect on your surroundings. I will address this *ONENESS* more in the Level Four class.

What are the Level Two, Three, and Four Classes Going to Teach You?

*It is not in the stars to hold our destiny
but in ourselves.*
-WILLIAM SHAKESPEARE

William Shakespeare was right when he said, "we hold our destiny in our own hands". Since our lives are about the journey itself, we have always something new to explore and evolve to. The following seminars are designed to support you in your expansion and elevate you to the next level. Please keep in mind learning how to access someone else's Akashic Records will not only enable you to support others, but will also give you a richer understanding of the incredible depths you will reach with this work.

Akashic Records Level Two:
How to Access Someone Else's Akashic Records

Course Description
Upon completion of this intensive class, you will be able to:
- skillfully give readings for others
- let go of contracts and attachments
- implement special techniques to change your DNA by using the advanced Grace Points
- find the origin of your "client's" health issues, patterns, and challenges and how to assist him or her in creating a more beneficial outcome
- align, balance, and uplift others through the spirit of the Akashic Records
- work from a space of unconditional love and compassion, which will act as a great blessing to you as well as those you serve
- learn how to channel the information received vibrationally through your fourth chakra rather than only using words

This class is appropriate for students who have successfully completed the Level One class.

Akashic Records Level Three:
How to Use the Guidance of the Akashic Records to Create an Energetic Healing Shift for Yourself and Someone Else

You will work on shifting energy by revealing and eliminating the roots of an issue or a challenge in order to achieve healing on all levels and create a harmonious life for yourself and your clients.

Course Description
Upon completion of this intensive class you will be able to:
• shift energy on the DNA level
• understand the importance of your subconscious mind and how to use it to heal unwanted patterns and create what you really want in your life as well as your clients' lives
• release issues on a karmic level
• release spirit attachments and energetic cords
• let go of false mental beliefs and emotional issues

This class is appropriate for students who have successfully completed the Level One and Two class.

Akashic Records Level Four:
How to Feel as One with God, the Source, and Creation

Course Description
You will work on shifting energy for yourself and your clients by revealing and eliminating separation from our source. Upon completion of this intensive class you will be able to:
• understand the interconnectedness of all beings, events, and things and explore your role in this field
• shift your cellular structure
• consciously create peace in your life
• define the qualities of oneness
• create and maintain your connection to God/Oneness/Source
• see your Akashic Record clients, and everybody else, as part of this oneness and wholeness

Certified Teacher Training Program

Transform your life, enrich your practice, and make a magnificent impact upon the world!

- Become the best Akashic Records Practitioner you can possibly be!
- Enrich your understanding and cultivate your connection with your own Akashic Records.
- Discover your leadership potential through the Akasha Records.
- Develop and refine your skills, receptivity, discernment and ability to work with others in an interdependent relationship.
- Use the Akashic Records as a stand-alone spiritual resource for personal empowerment and consciousness development.
- Access the Akashic Records to complement your already existing practices.
- Follow your deep desire to serve others as a Certified Teacher of this work.

This is a unique opportunity to train with Rev. Gabrielle Orr in the field of Akashic Records, who specializes in the use of the Akashic Records for personal empowerment and transformation.

As a graduate of this program you will be recognized as one of a select group entitled to teach the Gabrielle Orr method of accessing the Akashic Record.

Future Projects

*Acknowledging the good that you already have in your life
is the foundation for all abundance.*
-ECKHART TOLLE

Rev. Orr is currently working on a book about healing and spiritual intelligence in the Akashic Records, which includes her own experiences, healings with her clients, and transformations that happen during the Akashic Record classes. For more information, join her mailing list on her website, www.GabrielleOrr.com.

Recommended Reading

Application of Impossible Things: My Near Death Experience in Iraq by Natalie Sudman

Awakening the Power of a Modern God: Unlock the Mystery and Healing of Your Spiritual DNA and *The God Code* by Gregg Braden
New York Times best-selling author Gregg Braden is internationally renowned as a pioneer in bridging science, spirituality, and the real world.

The Biology of Belief: Unleashing the Power of Consciousness, Matter & Miracles by Bruce H. Lipton, PhD

The Field: The Quest for the Secret Force of the Universe by Lynne McTaggart

Science and the Akashic Field: An Integral Theory of Everything and *The Akashic Experience: Science and the Cosmic Memory Field* by Ervin Laszlo

Nominated for the Nobel Peace Prize in 2004 and 2005, Laszlo is the author of seventy-four books, such as *Science and the Akashic Field and Science and the Reenchantment of the Cosmos* and *The Systems View of the World: a Holistic Vision for Our Time.*

Notes

1. "Aether," *Wikipedia*, http://en.wikipedia.org/wiki/ Aether. According to ancient and medieval science, aether (Greek αἰθήρ), also spelled æther or ether, is the material that fills the region of the universe above the terrestrial sphere.

2. Quote from the book *"Science and the Akashic Field: An Integral Theory of Everything"*, by Ervin Laszlo

3. The eighth Chakra, the Universal Heart completes the octave of our personality-based consciousness and which is the portal to our higher transpersonal awareness. From a physical perspective, the eighth chakra, unlike the other seven major chakras, does not reside on the body. Instead, it hovers over the top of the body, above the crown chakra located at the highest point of the head. During the eighth chakra opening, the individual experiences a powerful spiritual shift. This brings with it a new

spiritual awareness that encompasses everything in an individual's life and can bring about great personal, professional, mental, and emotional changes. An open chakra of this type helps the individual to see his or her interconnectedness with all life and opens a portal to deeper spiritual and creative understanding.

4. Paganism: any of various religions other than Christianity or Judaism or Islam. In general Pagans include people who are on a spiritual path and don't conform to a major world religion.

5. The matrix is the base in which or from which things develop, the intercellular substance of a tissue from which a structure develops.

6. www.rsarchive.org. Anthroposophy is a road to knowledge, leading the spiritual part of the human being to the spirit of the universe.

7. Chakras are energy centers located in your body, mainly along your spine. It is believed that each chakra is connected to our being on several different levels: physical, emotional, mental, and spiritual. On the physical level, each chakra governs a main organ or gland, which is then connected to other body parts that resonate at the same frequency.
The color associated with the heart chakra is green. The heart chakra is of vital importance. It circulates love, balance, and compassion and keeps your immune system strong and powerful.

8. Pain-body

The word pain-body comes from the philosophy of Eckhart Tolle. A pain-body is the collective manifestation of all the pain, misery, and sorrow a person has ever gone through their entire life, including all the things they inherited from their culture and family history as well. A person's pain-body feeds and strengthens itself by making themselves and others miserable.

About the Author

After earning a degree in social work in Germany, Gabrielle Orr worked for several years with mentally disadvantaged children and coma patients. Her responsibilities included providing guidance as a life counselor for her clients and their families.

Today, Rev. Gabrielle Orr is a certified Akashic Record Teacher and Consultant, healing touch practitioner, reiki master, body talk practitioner, EFT practitioner, massage therapist, and feng shui consultant. She has been teaching Akashic Records classes and retreats internationally since 2002.

As a certified Akashic Records Teacher, Rev. Gabrielle Orr is a resourceful and intuitive teaching professional, highly trained in a wide variety of metaphysical studies.

She is talented at helping students open their hearts, feel confident, and maintain an open mind. She has proven her ability to maintain a highly-motivated and interactive class environment.

Rev. Gabrielle Orr offers individualized support and provides positive encouragement to ensure that each student succeeds.

As a collaborative educator with outstanding communication and interpersonal skills, she succeeds in cultivating and sustaining strong relationships within the class community.

Testimonials

Gabrielle,
I always feel like my soul has been cleansed after a session with you. :)
Since the class I took with you, I am more in tune with the Records myself and practice the things you taught me. It gives me a whole new perspective and often validates what I am already feeling.
I love you and appreciate you so much.
Lisa

My life, before & after Gabrielle Orr 's classes:
Your teachings have been key to my path. Since the day I took the very first class with you, my life changed. There's not one second in my life where I don't go deep

within and ask my heart "which way?" and there I go. The akashic records felt so "right". They have become my instant-to-instant practice.
Muchos besos & tons of blessings
Joan Z.

Guidance through class 1:
Dear Gabrielle,
Thank you for guiding me through class 1.
It was a wonderful experience, for my higher good!
I allow it. I allow it, I allow it.
Lina K.

Thank you Gabrielle!
I have published my book a few weeks ago and sold many copies to alternative practitioners and doctors. The cool thing is that a copy went to Malaysia, Ireland, Canada, Hawaii and 24 other states. I have been invited to Maine, possibly Canada, and here locally to teach this as a class. Your guidance was such a blessing. It gave me the confidence and the "wind under my wings" so I could fly. So thank you so much for seeing in me what I was still stretching into.
Catherine

Open up my heart:
I feel that meeting you enabled me to open up my heart more, be a more mindful person and look forward to my future with anticipation. Thank you very much for your awareness, genuine touch and sincerity.
Dominique

With much Love and Caring,
Gabrielle Orr

http://www.GabrielleOrr.com
http://www.facebook.com/GabrielleOrr

Your Personal Notes

Your Personal Notes

Your Personal Notes

Your Personal Notes

Your Personal Notes

Your Personal Notes

9 780615 843711